War S

*A collection of slang and other words
used in the Royal Air Force
during and after the 1939 – 45 war*

Remembered by Jean and Bernard Beadle
(2115686 LACW Beadle J F and 1323197 Cpl. Beadle B G F)

with additions suggested by ex-RAF friends

Tommies Guides

Tommies Guides
13 Hunloke Avenue, Eastbourne, BN22 8UL
www.tommiesguides.co.uk

First published in 2007 by
Tommies Guides: The military book specialists
www.tommiesguides.co.uk

ISBN 978-0-9555698-0-7

Packaged on behalf of Tommies Guides by
Beadle Davies, 59 Wood Green, Witney, Oxon OX28 1DB

Typeset by
Windrush Publishing Services, Adlestrop, Moreton-in-Marsh,
Gloucestershire, GL56 0YN

Printed by Lightning Source, Milton Keynes, United Kingdom

Introduction

This book is dedicated to my wife Jean Beadle (née Harris), born two months after me 1923 and to whom I was extraordinarily happily married from 1945 until 2000. It was as much her memory as mine that enabled us to recall these expressions of which there are over 400. It was a labour of love for us both because it was in the RAF, in the service of our country, that we met and were married.

It is also dedicated to Jean's sister Nancy Horne, who in the early 1990's thought of the original idea merely as a book of expressions from her ATS service and asked Jean and I to contribute. When Nancy moved on to other interests we took over the project.

The job was finished, as far as we could go, in March 1995. Since then more and more have come back to us but when Jean died, the project was very much put on hold. Now I have revised the original and added additional definitions. This is the result.

It is not offered as a complete dictionary of RAF slang, there may be words and phrases used in the post war Air Force of which I know nothing. It is intended to be in the vernacular, as we remembered it, from our time in the service.

Acknowledgements

I must offer thanks to those others who have kindly helped us in the compilation of this collection of words, terms and expressions. I am especially grateful to Arnold Bolton and, in alphabetical order of surname, my good friends Bernard Benson, Jack Robinson, Jack Thompson and Rusty Waughman.

I am particularly grateful to my son Ross and his wife Carys for their very great assistance with the complexities of publishing, and to Ryan Gearing for the cover design he developed from my original idea.

Bernard Beadle
February 2007

By way of an apology

(After all, Jean was one of those WAAF's it was good to have about.)

A reader to-day might be appalled at the seemingly politically incorrect terminology that is used over and over again as if the RAF was an almost entirely male organisation. In attitude I think it was. It is true that, as the war went on, we had an increasing number of women in the service that did a wonderful job, freed men for postings abroad and were good to have about. They were at that time regarded as auxiliaries in a male dominated and male oriented service (after all, were they not members of the Women's Auxiliary Air Force).

A

Ack

When telephones first came into use the reception was not always
good. To ensure accuracy it was necessary to introduce a phonetic
alphabet, using in place of the actual letters, words which could not be
misinterpreted. In the original phonetic alphabet ack was the word for
the letter A. Hence anti-aircraft fire was shortened to Ack Ack but
even this was too long for general use, hence the adoption of Archie,
See entry

ACH

Aircraft Hand. Those at the very bottom of the pay scale (Group 5),
often with no trade training, were known as Aircraft Hands, their
'trade' being designated, for instance ACH/GD for Aircraft Hand
/General Duties (meaning the dogsbody). See Chain Gang.

A C Plonk

The airman (i.e. 'other rank') at the bottom of the pile. See Plonk.

Adj

Adjutant, the commanding officer's senior administrative assistant. On
large stations the administrative department could be large enough to
require an officer of higher rank. He would be the 'Wing Co Admin'.
See Wingco.

Air House

At one time the three services tended to run quite independently
of each other. Each had its own headquarters: the Admiralty (Royal
Navy), the War Office (Army) and the Air Ministry, (Royal Air Force).
Those service departments have now been subsumed into one
department, the Ministry (or Department) of Defence. While it
existed, the Air Ministry was known as the Air House.

Airman

The personnel of the Royal Air Force were in one or other of two
categories – officer (i.e. commissioned officer) or airman (other
ranks) The latter was a decided misnomer since, although all ranks

in the RAF knew that they might be required to fly, only a small proportion ever did. It was once estimated that for every one man in the sky there were at least ten on the ground to keep them flying. Someone had to maintain the aircraft, others had to organise equipment and, of great importance, men were needed to feed and pay them. It can be said that the Royal Air Force is almost unique among the services since its other ranks send their officers out to fight.

Air Works
Used when speaking of the Royal Air Force in a derogatory or scathing manner; not unusually it would have been preceded by the strongest expletive of the day and called *the bloody Air Works*.

Albatross
Accepted Air Force terminology was full of misnaming. The badge worn just below the shoulder on the sleeves of other ranks was believed by them to be not an eagle but an albatross. It gave a feeling of superiority to old sweats when they explained to rookies and outsiders the error of their ways if the bird was misidentified. Ironically, they were probably wrong as it was an eagle. Alternative expressions were Kitehawks or Shitehawks.

Archie
The anti-aircraft gunfire of World War I (See Ack). By the time of World War II it had become Flak.

Arrow Sharpener
Used when indicating the long service of an airman. It would be said that: '*He was in the air force when arrow sharpener was a group 1 trade*'. See Group.

Arse End Charlie
At the beginning of the war, when a bomber offensive was expected, patrols of fighter aircraft could be seen in the sky. A squadron would assemble in four 'vicks' of three (i.e. four flights of three aircraft in V formation) except that one of the tail flight would weave from side to side keeping a look out behind. It was soon realised that (a) those bomber hoards were not coming (b) that radar could give sufficient warning of the approach and (c) it was very expensive to keep all

these aircraft in the sky at one time when they could be scrambled at short notice. That 'weaver' was the Arse End Charlie. See also Tail End Charlie.

Arsy Tarsy
ACRC (Aviation Candidate's Reception Centre) in St John's Wood, London. Some of the buildings at Lord's Cricket Ground were used for the reception and for medical examinations and pay parades. On occasions, adventurous PT Instructors would take squads to play 'tip it and run' on the hallowed Lord's cricket pitch, a piece of ground not normally used. Their charges were told that they were now entitled to say they had played cricket at Lords.

B

Baling Out
One of the many technical terms from the flying function of the RAF which took on a similar meaning in other situations. Although strictly meaning the escape from a crashing aircraft using a parachute, it also came to refer to the departure from almost any situation but usually implying relief. For example, on one's impending departure from an RAF station: *I shall be baling out from this dump next week.'* or, on a pub-crawl for instance: *I vote we bale out of here and try the Cow and Compasses.'*

Balloonatic
The term used during World War I to describe all who handled the observation balloons of the time. When the Balloon Barrage (a protection against enemy aircraft) was created prior to World War II, it was to be expected that the colloquialism of that earlier conflict should be revived for all involved in Balloon Command.

Bang On
Originally, in operational flying jargon, this was meant to be spot on target. It moved, like so many air force expressions, into general use on the ground inferring that all was well. For example: *'Did you get your leave alright?' 'Yes.' 'Bang on mate.'*

Basher

A word added to a trade or place of work to describe one who did that job or worked in that place, e.g. instrument basher, equipment basher. *See also* Wallah. Also used by those who had served in India to describe any accommodation hut; from the typical building used to house troops in the sub-continent.

Battle Bowler

Steel helmet; given its name when introduced into the army in 1916 because of its supposed similarity to the then popular civilian headgear.

Battle Dress

Blue 'battledress', modelled on the army's pattern, was introduced during the war as more suitable as working clothing and for wearing under flying clothing. It was welcomed by 'other ranks', who had to clean their own brass buttons, by the absence of such fastenings. Then one's only 'blue' became best blue. See Best Blue.

Belinda

Affectionate name given by members of a balloon crew to their balloon barrage charge.

Bender

A (usually very) alcoholic pub-crawl, normally in male company, though occasionally with female attachments.

Best Blue

'Other ranks' in wartime and before the arrival of blue battledress, were issued with two tunics and two pairs of trousers. Best blue referred to the tunic and trousers most recently issued; that is, the suit in better condition. It was kept for special occasions, full dress parades for instance, in particular when going on leave, going out on the town or when trying to 'pick up a bird'. When exchanging a suit comprising tunic and trousers for battledress you could be sure that the most worn would be handed in.

Bind

As a noun, generally meaning bore, wearisome or something that is either, '*This job is a right bind*' or talking of night watch (11 p.m. to

8 a.m.) *'I'm on night bind.'* Also used as a verb in, for example, *'He's binding on again,'* when he is being a bore or, possibly, *'opening the hangar doors'*. Hence binder, one who binds, though not always in a strongly derogatory sense.

Bint
Any, but usually young and particularly good looking, woman. As in so many service terms it derives from the British forces service in the Middle and Far East, coming from the Arabic *bint*, meaning daughter.

Biscuits
Small, hard mattress units, 2 feet 6 inches (76cm) square and about three inches (8cm) thick. Three made a full-length mattress for a single bed, but there were many times when they were just laid on the floor.

Black Outs
During the war it was a requirement that not a single peep of light should emanate from door or window lest the proliferation of the small rays might become something which an enemy bomber could identify as a town. All windows had to be covered with either black-out curtains or black-out screens. Thus, when WAAFs were issued with navy blue knickers it was inevitable that they became known, unofficially of course, as black outs. Originally made of dark flannel, later they were made in a softer grey material. Nevertheless, the name stuck. See *also* Passion Killers.

Blanco
Taken from the trade name (derived from the French *blanc* for white). It was used to whiten webbing equipment once worn by British soldiery. When, in the interests of camouflage, webbing equipment was required to be khaki the name prevailed and 'khaki blanco' was used. For RAF webbing equipment we had 'blue blanco'.

Blighty
Home, Britain. From the Hindustani *bilayati*, foreign land. The object of many a nostalgic thought in the mind of a serviceman abroad.

Blood Wagon
An ambulance.

Blower
The telephone. Whether this came from Civvy Street to the services or vice versa does not appear to be known.

Blue Eyes
See Front Teeth.

Bod
Abbreviation of body, i.e. a person.

Boffin
A scientist. Almost always a civilian involved in research and development of any piece of service equipment. In the RAF this meant war planes, armaments, radar etc.

Bogey
An enemy aircraft. Not the objectionable green thing which was wont to dangle from the nostril of one with a pretty heavy cold but something much more down to earth, though equally objectionable.

Bought It
A euphemism, with no relation to purchasing something. 'He's bought it,' means that he has been killed, usually in a plane crash, or has been shot down with the same result.

Brassed Off
Fed up. Similar to cheesed off. Frequently expanded to 'Brassed off with…' or 'Brassed off about…' It had a stronger version, Pissed off, or stronger still, Bloody well pissed off. An interesting past tense of the stronger version was 'He peed me off.'

Brown Job
To a member of the RAF, any soldier in the army of any rank. Not to be mistaken for Brown Nose. See also Pongo, Squaddie and Swaddie.

Brown Nose
Someone who crawls to a superior. An allusion to the deposit on his nose which might have accrued from the orifice where (metaphorically) it had been.

Bristols
From the Cockney rhyming slang Bristol Cities, the upper front portion of a woman's torso.

Brylcreem Boys
Mildly slanderous but inaccurate nickname, given to members of the RAF by other servicemen and civilians. The origin is not known though it has been suggested that because the RAF's 'other ranks' tended to walk beside their caps (see forage cap), i.e. almost resting on their right ears. Brylcreem on the hair was supposedly needed as a fixative.

Buckshee
Free, spare. From the Hindustani *baksheesh*, meaning, gratuity. Like so many words of service slang, originating from the British army's service in India.

Bull Shit
Derived from the notion that the excrement of a bull was, or was considered to be, of no use, just rubbish. The term meant just that, rubbish. For instance, told a lot of duff gen (see Gen) one would say, 'That's a load of bull shit.' Any 'spit and polish' regarded as being over the score or unnecessary was bullshit. Note: bullshit was frequently shortened to bull. Polishing one's boots was bulling them. See Oxometer.

Bumph (or bumf)
Any, normally official, paperwork. Even so much as one short letter could evince the comment, 'God, more bloody bumph'. The origin is pretty obvious, the roll of paper found hanging in the 'smallest room'.

Burton
See Gone for a Burton

C

Camp Comedian
Some RAF establishments would have been the home of several units, each with its own commanding officer. The officer in charge was known as the Camp Commandant, but if a large unit might have had a section of it based elsewhere, then the administrative head of that establishment would be called the Camp Comedian.

Canteen Cowboy
A ladies' man. Presumably because he was observed making his first advances in the canteen, on a station or in the nearby town.

Ceremonial Belt
Part of an airman's equipment was a set of webbing bits and pieces similar to those issued to the army. For special occasions the waist belt was worn alone. Before the war a special version of this was issued for use on ceremonial occasions. It had no buckles at the back and, usually, had to be Blancoed white (see Blanco). There was a secondary meaning, successful fornication on the parade ground.

Chain Gang
Probably the lowest in the estimation of their fellows, the ACH/GHDs (aircraft hand general duties) found themselves doing the most menial tasks, hence the comparison with convict labour. See ACH.

Char
Taken into English from the Urdu (Hindustani) for tea, char, or from the Chinese ch'a. One of the many words brought back to this country by servicemen returning from India. Hence char wallah, one who made or sold cups of tea.

Char and Wad
A cuppa and a sandwich, cake, bun or scone. See Wad.

Charpoy
A bed. Nothing whatsoever to do with char (tea). Again from the Hindustani.

Cheese Cutter

Peaked cap. In wartime issued only to service police and motor transport drivers. Although officers and warrant officers wore peaked caps as part of their uniform the term was used only in relation to the headgear of 'other ranks'.

Cheesed Off

Origin unknown, a version of Brassed Off.

Chiefy

Flight sergeant. Normally used only when addressing a close associate, one under whom you worked, or one with whom you were on social terms.

Chips

Originally a term from the USA and first recorded in print as long ago as 1819. It was in frequent war time use as a noun in conjunction with the verbs to have and to get. Indicating beaten, finished or (rarely) killed, 'He's had his chips' could mean he has been found out, is not going to get the leave he had hoped for or even that he is not going to 'make it' with his current girl friend. In the extreme case it could signify that he is dead but other terms were more usual. See Bought It or Had It.

Chit

A short note or a receipt. To be excused duties, for instance, one had to have a chit. Another word resulting from the British army's service in India, it comes from the Hindustani *citta*, a note.

Chocks Away

An aircraft, when parked, has triangular shaped chocks in front of and behind its wheels to prevent it rolling. Before it could take off one of the ground staff would remove them and call out to the pilot '*Chocks away*'. So it came to its general meaning, '*Let's get started*'.

Circuits and Bumps

Training exercise for pilots in which they would (just) touch down then take off, circle and do the whole thing again. A chap stooging around, not appearing to get anywhere, would have it said of him: '*What's he doing, circuits and bumps?*'

Civvie

Civilian or a civilian. To be 'in civvies' was to be in civilian clothing instead of uniform. Interestingly the RAF did not appear to have taken the army's term mufti when it became a separate force in 1918.

Civvie Street

The life, place of work or home of a civilian.

Click, To

1. To make acquaintance with a member of the opposite sex.
2. One could also click a leave pass (pleasant) or click for a guard duty (the opposite).

Coffin Nails

Cheaper and rougher cigarettes, often ascribed to 'Wild Woodbines' which were among the cheapest cigarettes.

At the beginning of the war, most cigarettes were priced at six pence for ten and a shilling for twenty. 'Wild Woodbines' made by W D & H O Wills and 'Weights' made by Players retailed at tuppence for five and four pence for ten.

Commissioned Crumpet

A particularly good looking WAAF officer. In the Royal Navy they were rather more polite, calling them Commissioned Lovelies.

Conductor

Navigator cum radar operator in two-seater night fighters, the Mosquito or Beaufighter. The crew consisted of Driver and Conductor.

Confined to Camp (CC)

The RAF equivalent of the army's CB (confined to barracks). See Jankers.

Cooler

A cell in the guardroom. The services equivalent of the civilian police cell. In prisoner of war camps it was a cell for the solitary confinement of recaptured escapees when they were returned.

Corp.

Familiar term for corporal but normally used by those of lower rank only to this junior NCO when he was personally known, i.e. as in charge of his section.

Crowned

When a sergeant was promoted to the next higher rank, flight sergeant, he wore a crown above his three stripes (correctly called chevrons). On that promotion he was said to have been crowned.

Cuppa

Although assumed to be a contraction of 'a cup of' it is more specifically a short form of 'a cup of tea'. A cuppa would not normally contain coffee, cocoa or any beverage other than tea.

Cushy

Easy, pleasant. From the Hindustani *khush*, pleasant. For example, '*He's got a cushy number*' means that he has a comfortable job.

CWF

Correctly ACH/CWF. Chemical warfare fighter. Some GDs were given what many considered rudimentary training in poison gasses which might be used, their effects and how to combat them. In small units a sergeant ACH/CWF might double as, in effect, Station Warrant Officer.

D

Dekko

More properly dekho. From the Hindustani *dekho* to look and *dekhna* to see.

Desert Lily

A home-made urinal. Devised in the desert of North Africa, it was contrived from two 4 gallon tin plate petrol cans, both with holes in their bases and tops removed. The lower stood vertically with its base settled into the ground. The upper sat in it at an angle. It was regarded as essential for hygiene.

Digititis
A common admonition when requiring a person to get on with a job was 'Get your finger out'. Similarly, when one was not getting on with a job he was described as having finger trouble. A digit being a finger, a sluggard was described as having digititis. See Finger.

Dim View
Something which one took when not viewing or regarding with any approval.

Diver
The first of the German terror weapons, followed by the V2 rocket. Fortunately the V3 was not developed in time to be used before the end of the war. See VI.

Dixie
Large oval shaped metal pot with lid and carrying handle used for cooking. The pot could be used for making stew etc or brewing tea. The lid doubled as a frying pan. From the Hindustani *degchi* small pot.

Dobhi
Hindustani for washing clothes. Hence doing one's dobhi or dobhi walla, the chap who does your laundry for you.

Dock
Hospital or Station Sick Quarters.

Dodging the Column
Shirking. The art of avoiding particularly dangerous or unpleasant duties. The expression originated in India and South Africa, a column being a body sent forward into hostile territory.

Doodlebug
See Diver and VI.

Drill
Not just the physical movements made on the parade ground. Drill came to mean the correct way of setting about a job. 'OK, you've got the job to do but do you know the drill?'

Drink, In the
Drink usually means the sea though it can be a lake. '*In the drink*' inferred that an aircraft had come down in water or that its pilot and crew had parachuted into the sea. Because this was an unpleasant experience, the term came to be used in a wider sense for example, when retribution was about to be forthcoming.

Driver
Not necessarily one in charge of a motor vehicle (normally called a DMT – Driver, Motor Transport). The term was one of distinction given to the pilot of a large aircraft.

Duff
Usually as an adjective before gen indicating of poor standard: '*Don't you believe it, it's just duff gen.*'

E

Ear 'ole
Considered to be a polite euphemism for 'arse hole', a crawler. '*He's a right ear 'ole*' was considered more acceptable in certain company than, for instance, '*God, 'e's climbing up 'is bloody arse 'ole.*'

Elsan
The chemical toilet. Well known to campers and always provided in bomber and coastal command aircraft. Used as an adjective before 'gen' to indicate unreliability. '*Don't you believe it, that's real Elsan gen.*'

Erk
Originally a naval term for 'rating'. It was adopted by the RAF, probably at the amalgamation of the RFC and the RNAS in 1918, for the lowest rank, aircraftsman, even up to the highest grade in that rank (during World War II, leading aircraftsman). For example, '*This whole section is run by erks*' implied that it had no NCO in charge or was ineffectual. Interestingly this was a wholly male term, never used about WAAFs.

ET pack

ET was an abbreviation for early treatment. The ET pack was an anti-VD pack available to those returning from a doubtful encounter.

F

FFI

Free from infection. It described the inspection by a medical officer or medical orderly of a man's 'privates' to check that he was free from infection by venereal disease. It was usually required on arrival at a new station or unit and, very often, on returning from leave. Also known as a Short Arm Inspection.

Finger Trouble

A person having difficulty or not getting on with a job was deemed to have finger trouble and would be instructed to get his finger out. The rather crude origin of the term is left to the reader's imagination. *See* Digititis.

Firkin

The RAF's universal noun, not to be mistaken for the serviceman's expletive which had a different first vowel sound. Take as an example the exchange between an engine fitter, up on a scaffold, and his mate on the ground:

> *'Gi's that firkin, will you.'*
> *'This firkin?' holding up some tool.*
> *'No, the other firkin.'*

The word was only used, of course, when the two in conversation had a pretty good idea of what was being referred to. *See also* Gubbins

Fizzer

A charge, or the Form 252 on which the disciplinary offence was detailed. It was completed when an 'other rank' had, or was accused of having, transgressed some article of service law. Usually it followed 'On a...'

Flag Wagging

In the Royal Navy, signalling either by semaphore or by signal flags. In the RAF the ritual of raising the flag at dawn (or reveille) and its lowering as sun set. A performance carried out only on a station whose CO liked Bull and was well away from the firing line.

Flak

The 'archie' or 'Ack Ack' fire of World War I became flak by World War II from the German *fliegerabwehrkanone*, anti-aircraft gun. It came to mean being on the receiving end of (probably well merited) verbal abuse, particularly from a superior. For instance: '*I got a load of flak thrown at me!*'

Flak Happy

Aircrew who had been considered too stressed to continue flying on operations. Subsequently used to describe anyone mentally disturbed. *See* LMF.

Flap

A state of panic. It also meant when something had to be done in an almighty hurry, possibly for the unanticipated arrival of a person of importance.

Flea Pit

Originally a sleeping bag. Later used for any bed, however made up. Probably originated from the menace of fleas on the body which settled in a made-up bed awaiting the occupant's return. Also used to describe a small local cinema.

Fling One Up

To salute. '*Here comes an officer, fling one up for him.*'

Flush

Irreverent collective noun for a group of Wing Commanders (W/Cs). The commanding officer of an RAF station was normally a Group Captain who had officers of the next lower rank in charge of sections, i.e. Wingco Flying, Wingco Engineering, Wingco Admin.

When, periodically, they came together for a meeting it could be described as a Flush of WCs.

Flying Arsehole

When military flying began in 1914, aircraft were used as spotters. The second crewman was an observer and differentiated from the pilot by wearing a half brevet on his tunic, with a single winged letter O which became known as the Flying Arsehole. The war over, this award was discontinued but in the mid-30's navigation was seen as a specialist task rather than being left to the pilot. Initially the new breed of navigators was awarded the old Observer brevet. Early in World War II all aircrew were accorded a brevet when the N (Navigator) and AG (Air Gunner) were introduced.

Forby, Four-by-Two

A piece of flannelette cloth that size (in inches), oiled and pulled through the barrel of a rifle to clean it.

Form OO

The army had devised forms for all manner of communication. When the RAF was created it took over rather more from the army than the navy. However Form OO referred to those rolls of paper hung on the wall of the 'smallest room'. Service issue tended to be rough on one side and smooth on the other. Said the wags, 'Universal, mate, smooth for officers' bums, coarse for 'other ranks' arses'.

Freeman, Hardy & Willis

At the time a well known chain of shoe shops, but here referring to certain medals. Another name for the three World War I 'gongs' better known as Pip, Squeak and Wilfred. Those who served abroad up to the end of 1915 received either the 1914 or 1914/15 star. For others there was the star covering service from 1916 to the end of hostilities and the Victory Medal.

Front Teeth

In no way connected with dentistry. A young lady of substantial, or even just delightful, upper proportions was said to have – well let me quote: 'Just look at those two front teeth.' See also Blue Eyes, Bristols.

Fruit Salad

Medal ribbons. Usually reserved for a display consisting of more than one row.

G

GD
The lowest trade classification for 'other ranks', correctly ACH/GD, aircraft hand, general duties; an airman with no trade training. *See* Chain Gang.

Gen
Probably a contraction of genuine, strictly knowledge or true information, as opposed to rumour. Sometimes employed to suggest what was NOT actually true. Also used as an adjective in place of genuine or some similar synonym, e.g. 'He's a gen bloke'. Note also Duff Gen (useless or inaccurate information) and Pukka Gen.

Get Some Flying Hours In
Sleeping. A person feeling tired could say to his mates, '*I'm going to get some flying hours in*'. Alternatively, a mate in the same hut who would insist on talking after lights out would be commanded, in no uncertain terms, to '*Get some flying hours in!*'

Glasshouse
Army or RAF military prison or detention centre. The term came from the army's detention barracks at Aldershot which had a glass roof.

Gnat's
Abbreviation of gnat's piss. Described a cup of weak tea as opposed to a stronger brew called 'Sergeant Major's'.

Gravel Bashing
Drill. See Square Bashing. Hence gravel basher – drill instructor.

Gremlin
The mythical creature which has been responsible for an almost, or at first, unexplainable fault. For example, '*Bloody gremlins again.*'

Grocer
The equipment officer, responsible for ordering and having on hand all items of equipment, supplies, clothing etc. which may be required.

God Squad

Something of which you were said to be a member if you showed strong religious convictions. In a derogatory sense it indicated those Roman Catholics who used their obligation to attend mass every Sunday. On night watch, for instance, when finishing at 8 a.m. they would find it necessary to attend the seven o'clock service whereas when on day duty or on morning watch they would arrive at work late having attended at eight o'clock. Comment typically made on their arrival, but not always in their hearing: *'Here comes the (strong adjective occasionally) God Squad.'*

Golden Eagle

The golden eagle lays its eggs on Friday – i.e. *'Today is pay day!'* In common parlance the four letter word for excreta sometimes replaces lays its eggs.

Gone for a Burton

Named after the town in which it was brewed, Burton was a favourite ale in England in the thirties and forties. To say that a chap had gone for a Burton was to suggest that his absence was due to him having gone to the bar to buy a beer, but in fact, it was a euphemism for being killed. The term was later used for anything that had been destroyed, aircraft, vehicle or building. Synonyms: Bought It, 'Ad It.

Gongs

Decorations (orders, crosses, or medals) awarded for gallantry, conspicuous service or for participating in a campaign. See Naafi Gong.

Group

A formation in the airforce. Originally and generally three planes constituted a flight, three flights made a squadron, several squadrons together made a wing and wings were assembled into groups. Actual numbers could vary as operational and administrative necessity required. The term was also used to indicate the degree of skill (and the pay rates) of airmen. At the top, in Group 1, were the highest, wireless mechanics, airframe and engine fitters etc. At the bottom, in Group 5, were those whose jobs required little or no skill.

Gubbins

An alternative to Firkin.

H

Had It
The meaning varies with the person or the preceding verb. In the second person, 'You've had it' or, to add strength, 'You've bloody had it', implies that neither were you in possession in the past nor are you going to be in the future, e.g.: 'Sergeant, can I have some time off?' 'You've bloody had that mate.'

In the first person there is either an implication that one is aware of not being successful or a statement of one's lack of success while the same can apply in the third person: eg 'He's had it' or 'They've had it'.

Half-pint Hero
A regular boaster. One who frequently opens the hangar doors, see below.

Hangar Doors
Shortened form of Opening the Hangar Doors, the cry of one's auditors when one is shooting a line or boasting.

Homework
A girl friend, almost always preceded by an appreciative adjective. 'She's a smashing bit of homework.'

Hussif
Corruption of housewife. The small pack of needles, thread, buttons etc. needed for minor repairs to one's kit.

I

Iron Lung
At one time the only way in which a sufferer from poliomyelitis could be kept alive was in an artificial breathing machine, nicknamed iron lung. It came to be used, though for no medical or medical related reason, to describe a Nissan hut, a prefabricated building with a semi circular cross-section constructed from sheets of corrugated iron and

standing on a low brick wall. With no insulation they were either very hot in summer or uncomfortably cold in winter.

Irons
Knife, fork and spoon issued to airmen and women below senior NCO rank. Usually it was carried in a pocket during working hours to save going back to one's billet to fetch them at meal times

It's One of Theirs
It's an enemy aircraft. Spoken during the London or other blitz it suggested that a person could tell by the engine noise that it was an enemy aircraft. The statement was invariably correct since the proportion of enemy to friendly aircraft was very much in favour of the former. In fact, there were few, if any, who could recognise foe or friend from engine noise save when the V1 Doodlebug campaign was being waged.

J

Jankers
The second grade of punishment awarded to an airman. It came between the lowest, 'admonition', and the highest, 'detention' in the glasshouse. Correctly called Confined to Camp (CC), it meant just that, confined to camp plus the requirement to report either to the guardroom or the unit orderly room first thing in the morning (before breakfast) in full kit (complete with webbing equipment). Reporting was also required, similarly dressed, after the evening meal, when two hours suitable work, mostly of a completely useless nature, was required.

Jerrican
Originally petrol was transported in four gallon cans made of tinplate. They proved to be vulnerable to pressure, for instance when stacked in too high a pile, and to almost any pointed object. The design used by the German forces was of steel and of a thicker gauge. Seen to be much more durable, and able to be reused, it was adopted by British, and later, all allied forces. It took its name from its origin, copied from the Jerries.

Jerry

At the start of World War I the term Hun was almost universally used for a German but towards the end Jerry had, in part, taken over. By the start of World War II the latter was almost universal. There is doubt as to whether the term came from 'German' or because their steel helmets were said to resemble chamber pots.

K

Kite

Not something children fly on the end of a piece of string. An aircraft.

Kitehawk

See Albatross.

L

LMF

Lacks moral fibre. The diagnosis given to a flier, a member of an aircrew, who could not take the mental strain of continuous danger, rather more than just Flak Happy. He was usually deprived of his air-crew brevet, reduced to the ranks and posted to another station.

M

Mae West

A Hollywood actress of the thirties and forties who was endowed rather handsomely above the waist. The life saving jacket, worn by pilots of fighter aircraft in case of Pancaking In The Drink, gave them a rather busty look. Hence the comparison. It is interesting that a slang term has become the official description of this piece of safety equipment.

Meat Wagon
Ambulance. *See also* Blood Wagon

Mutt and Jeff
The pair of Great War campaign medals – British War Medal and Victory Medal – awarded to those who served from 1916 onwards. They were named after the cartoon characters created originally in the United States by Bud Fisher but popular in Great Britain by 1920, the time when campaign medals were being sent out. *See also* Pip, Squeak and Wilfred.

N

NAAFI
Navy, Army and Air Force Institute. The organisation which maintained canteens, principally for those below senior NCO rank. On bases where there was family accommodation it provided mini-supermarket facilities.

Naafi Gong
The first of the World War II campaign medals, the 1939/45 Star. It was awarded, generally, for six months service in a war zone, but that time could be spent at a base unit far from any scene of conflict. Because it was additional to stars awarded for service in particular theatres it was the most common. Hence the, in the main, undeserved derogatory nickname. *See also* Spam Medal

Nobby
At one time the name given to men working as clerks. It came to be the nickname for anyone with that surname even if spelled Clark. It is believed to originate from the fact that clerks in offices, to demonstrate their having a status above that of ordinary workmen, wore top hats rather than the cloth cap or bowler of those they considered inferior. But top hats were the head gear of the nobs (the upper classes), hence their being called nobbies.

O

Old Sweat

One, usually an 'Other Rank', who had got some in, i.e. had been in the service for a good number of years. In wartime such a person was said to have been: *In the Airworks since Pontius was a pilot'*.

On the Peg

See Peg.

Organise

Not just to get things in order, more often to get something on the cheap, at no cost, or to obtain when strictly not entitled. For instance:
'You off home?'
'Yes.'
'How d'you do it?'
'Organised some sick leave'.

Other Ranks (ORs)

Airmen, those in ranks below commissioned officer.

Oxometer

During World War II Blackpool was very largely taken over by the RAF to accommodate training units, principally for recruits. The celebrated Blackpool Tower was used as a radar station, an aerial being erected on its top. This impressive array was known colloquially in the town as 'the oxometer', the instrument supposedly used by the Air Commodore commanding the station to measure the amount of Bull Shit being generated.

P

Packet

Originally a wound. Hence, to 'Cop a Packet' was to suffer a wound, often fatal. It also indicated, at one extreme, that one had been caught out doing something wrong or, at the other extreme, it was also applied to one who caught a venereal disease.

Padre

The familiar term for a chaplain. From the Latin *pater*, father.

Pancake

Land with undercart still retracted.

Passion Killers

WAAF's knickers, typical of the fashion of the day and not particularly modeish, they had elasticated legs. The name was given by those who wished to 'explore'.

Peg

On the Pegs was a colloquial expression for being on a charge (see Fizzer). This was not to be mistaken for the petrol electric generator that was the bane of a wireless operator's life when serving on a mobile unit. Then the PEG consisted of a small two-stroke engine attached to an electrical generator, which kept batteries charged. If the PEG stopped it required immediate attention, easy during the day when there was an off-watch wireless operator, but at night time it meant the duty operator signing off to attend to the machine by the light of a torch, usually some distance away.

Penguin

A non-flying officer.

Piece of Cake

Normally, an easy job, task or assignment, something easily done but not infrequently used as a comment made out of modesty when a difficult task had been accomplished.

'That was a bloody good job you did.'
'No, it was a piece of cake.'

Pip, Squeak & Wilfred

The trio of World War I medals, Mutt & Jeff preceded by the 1914 or 1914–15 Star. Named after the popular cartoon characters in the *Daily Mirror*. See Freeman, Hardy and Willis.

Pissed off

See Brassed Off.

Pit

Bed. See Flea Pit.

Plonk

Not the poorest quality of wine but the general term used for an airman of the lowest grade. An AC2 (Aircraftsman second class) was referred to as AC Plonk.

Plumber

An airman in the trade of armourer.

Pongo

A member of the RAF's term for an army officer, usually of low rank.

Pontius Pilate

A long serving officer or airman or even a piece of antiquated equipment was said to have been in the Air Force *'since Pontius was a pilot'*.

Prang

Normally used in the past tense, pranged or sometimes had a prang. Initially it was used exclusively about a crashed aircraft but, like so many terms, it gradually took on a wider meaning and could be applied to almost anything damaged or destroyed. But see Wizard Prang which had a quite different meaning.

Prune

The personification of stupidity or incompetence. The term comes from Pilot Officer Prune, a character in the aircrew training manual who frequently behaved in an idiotic fashion; e.g. 'He's a right prune'.

PT

Officially physical training, but it was also a euphemistic form for a young lady who may have a somewhat provocative and flirtatious manner, but would pull down the shutters rather than her knickers. From p…k teaser.

Pull Through

Often used to describe a tall thin person. The slang term comes from the device supplied with every rifle, a weighted string having a loop at its other end. A piece of oiled Four by Two was attached and pulled through the barrel of a rifle to clean it.

Q

Queen Bee

The senior WAAF officer on an RAF station or unit.

Queen Mary.

A long, low articulated vehicle used for carrying aircraft, generally to or from a maintenance unit or other repair depot. It might also carry the remains of a crashed aircraft either for repair or to a dump for reclamation of bits still useable. In its time it was probably one of the longest vehicles on the road.

R

Raff

The usual and simple pronunciation of RAF.

> 'John's been called up.'
> 'In the army?'
> 'No, he's in the Raff.'

Records Glos.

The RAF's Records Office was in Gloucester. From it emanated signals ordering the posting of airmen or WAAFs below commissioned rank to different stations. In a station's signals office it could not help but be noticed that far more of these signals ordered a posting abroad. Hence the cry from the duty teleprinter operator: *'It's from Records Glos; who's the poor devil going overseas now?'*

Red Cap

A military policeman. So called because of the red top to his peaked cap. Though a soldier, he had jurisdiction over all military personnel, army, navy or airforce. See *SP*. Note, RAF police wore white tops to their caps and eventually acquired the nick name, Snowdrops.

Rookie

A new recruit, usually in his/her period of initial disciplinary training, but sometimes used for very newly qualified tradesmen, e.g. *'We've got two rookie fitters just arrived in the section'*.

Roger

Used in radio telephonic (R/T) communication, i.e. by voice as opposed to Morse Code, meaning message received and understood. Having the same meaning it came to be used in everyday parlance. *See also* Willco.

S

Sally Ann

Salvation Army. A wonderful organisation which provided material comforts for the troops, often in quite dangerous situations. It was better known by members of the forces for the welfare rather than the religious side of its work.

Schoolie

An education officer. Usually, during the war, a graduate teacher with responsibility for running educational classes of an academic or mildly technical nature, organising talks on current affairs and providing advice on topics within his ken. The war over it was the job of education officers to run the EVT (Educational and Vocational Training) scheme aimed to better equip personnel for their return to civilian life.

Scramble
A genuine technical term used in Fighter command as an instruction to the waiting pilots to board their aircraft and get airborne as soon as possible. In the past tense it had a reporting function: '*604 squadron was scrambled*' or '*B Flight was scrambled at 06.30*'.

Scrambled Egg
The gold, leaf-shaped decoration, on the peak of an officer's cap, rank of Group Captain or above (RAF) and Commander or above (RN). During the war the army abandoned scrambled egg.

Sergeant Major's
Good and very strong tea. Derived from the comparison of tea with the urine of gnats at one end of the scale and that of sergeant-majors at the other: '*This is gnat's pee, give me a drop of good sergeant major's.*'

Scotch Mist
Along with whisky, new potatoes and eggs, the only thing that can correctly be described as Scotch, otherwise the adjective should be Scottish. In the airforce something which one should be able to see but apparently can't. Example, an NCO, ignored or having his instruction doubted would draw attention to his rank by pointing to his stripes and saying: '*What d'you think these are, Scotch mist?*'

Shitehawk
See Albatross.

Shit Hot
The absolute accolade; first rate in every sense, very good news. Example: '*He's a shit hot wireless operator.*'

Shooting a Line
See Hangar Doors.

Short Arm Inspection
See FFI. Derived from it being an inspection of a man's private parts.

Shot Down in Flames

Literally the end of an aircraft following a successful attack by fighter, a bomber's gunners or anti-aircraft fire. It was rarely used in that context within the RAF though it was beloved by journalists. Bought it was the more usual term in the service. Like so many RAF expressions it was used far more as a metaphor when describing the plight of a boaster who had been deflated, a person whose argument had been conclusively destroyed or of one who had been crossed in love.

Side Cap

More properly known as 'cap, field service', and more commonly known as the forage cap. It received this picturesque name because of the tendency for it to be worn well over to the right, almost resting on one's ear. It was said that in the RAF you didn't wear your cap, you walked alongside it. See Brylcreem Boys.

Silver Sausage

A barrage balloon, so called because they were made of silver coloured fabric. Could this colour have been chosen as a form of camouflage? One has to doubt it; rarely were the skies over Britain that colour.

Six Six Four B

During World War II, when all items of kit were issued, anything lost had to be replaced and paid for. To obtain that replacement and have its cost docked from pay, one of the service's innumerable forms had to be completed. To wit, Form 664B.

Skipper (Skip)

The captain (i.e. first pilot) of a large aircraft. No matter what ranks were held by other members of the crew the pilot was always the skipper.

Skirt Patrol

On the lookout for a bit of feminine company.

Sky Pilot

All three services used this term for a clergyman, though usually it was reserved for service chaplains. The only (apparent) flyer who did not wear an aircrew brevet. He was not a member of the flying branch. See Padre.

Snoop
Service policemen. See SP.

Snowdrop
Later in the war the name given to RAF police because of the white tops to their caps. Adopted from US usage; American military police wore white helmets.

SP
An RAF service policeman, the equivalent of a Military Policeman, MP.

Spam Medal
See Naafi Gong. Spam was a tinned meat product, with a basis of ham, produced in the United States. It was an alternative to Bully Beef (Corned Beef). Though regarded for its slight spiciness as an occasionally welcome change from the monotony of Bully, it was less highly regarded because of its somewhat blander taste.

Sparks
Originally referred to the sparks badge, worn on the upper right sleeve of airmen below the rank of warrant officer, indicating the trade of wireless operator or wireless mechanic. It was also the term used for one of these tradesmen: *'Hey, sparks, can you fix this radio for me?'* The badge is purported to have been introduced in the early days of the service when an airman was permitted to speak to an officer only through an NCO. The sparks badge allowed him to make the approach directly if, for instance, an urgent signal (message) had been received. When the trades of radar operator and radar mechanic were introduced they too were entitled to wear the badge but were not accorded the title.

Sprog
Having the same meaning as Rookie.

Squaddie
A soldier, usually below commissioned rank. It probably came from squad, a group of soldiers but it may have been a corruption of swaddy, an 18th century word for bumpkin.

Square Bashing
The early months of an airman's training, the so called discip. (disciplinary) course where drill predominated. Alternatively Pebble Bashing.

Station Master
Then the title of the official in charge of a railway station (now called the station manager) but in the RAF the unofficial title of the officer commanding an RAF station.

Station Warrant Officer (SWO)
Usually an ACH/GD, who had slowly progressed up through the ranks. He was the senior disciplinary 'other rank' on a station or large unit and he was usually regarded as the senior warrant officer but, in terms of remuneration, he collected less than tradesmen warrant officers, being in the lowest group (group 5) on the pay scales.

Stooging About
Flying, or any other activity, where there appeared to be no apparent motive for the action; for instance, using up time or hanging around aimlessly.

Strip
Off which one was torn when reprimanded by a superior. The believed derivation is the act of tearing off the stripes of an NCO reduced to the ranks for some serious misdemeanour.

Swaddie
See Squaddie.

Sweat
See Old Sweat.

SWO
See Station Warrant Officer.

T

Tail-end Charlie
Or, in more colloquial terms, Arse-end Charlie, the tail gunner of a bomber or heavy Coastal Command aircraft.

Tannoy
This firm appeared to have had the contract to provide public address equipment on all home RAF stations. Their loudspeakers were clearly marked with their name. Just as that so very useful domestic cleaning device has become generally known as a Hoover, irrespective of its manufacturer, so Tannoy became synonymous with public address.

Tapes
The chevrons worn on the upper sleeve denoting non-commissioned rank (corporal, sergeant, flight sergeant). On promotion to corporal it would be said, 'He's got his tapes'.

This comes from the custom, in India and other hot countries where shirts were laundered frequently. The official material insignia faded with washing. and chevrons of white tape were sewn on. in their place.

Target for Tonight
Strictly, of course, what it says: the destination of a bomber or bomber force during the coming hours of darkness. The term was used as the title of a film, made early in the war, depicting the work of Bomber Command. However, it was yet another of the RAF's technical terms which came to have an alternative meaning. It was sometimes the pub or other establishment at which one planned to spend some off duty time but more often it referred to the female companion with whom one hoped to (or was going to) spend an agreeable time.

Tate & Lyle
The badge of rank worn by a warrant officer on his lower sleeve. It was so called because it resembled the royal arms contained within the 'by appointment' on a tin of golden syrup manufactured by that company.

Teat (or Tit)

Any push button control be it bell push, camera trigger, gun button or bomb release.

Tee Up

Clearly from the game of golf, preparing for any task: *'You've got to fit that new transmitter, are you teed up?'*

Ticket

To get one's ticket was to get discharged from the service. Sometimes it was used, still in the sense of discharge, as when one hoped to leave sick quarters or a service hospital.

Toys

Mechanical parts of an aircraft or a gun. When a fitter or an armourer was working on the innards of a piece of equipment he was said to be playing with his toys.

Two Six!

Derivation unknown (to the compilers). Working on a flight dispersal and hearing this cry meant that ALL personnel, of whatever trade, were required for an emergency. It could be the onset of high winds which required lighter aircraft to be guyed down or because of some catastrophe which manpower could overcome – such as a light to moderate sized aircraft which had managed to get one wheel off the tarmac and which brute force could return to hard ground.

Type

A kind of person. An acceptable person would be a good type, alternatively, at the other extreme, a bolshie type, a ropey type or a useless type.

U

Undercart

An aircraft's undercarriage, its landing gear. Also the parts of a young lady below the hemline, e.g.: *'Cor, she's got a smashing undercart!'*

U/S
Not big brother on the other side of the Atlantic. Contraction of unserviceable, sometimes used to describe an inefficient workman or anything of poor quality.

U/T
Under training. During his training as a wireless operator an airman would have his trade shown as u/t w/op.

V

V1
The first of the German so called terror weapons, the V1 (vergeltungswaffen – vengeance weapon) was a pilotless aircraft, in effect a flying bomb. It was launched from the Pas-de-Calais region of France, principally against London. In official communiqués they were called divers and in common parlance, doodlebugs.

W

Wad
Properly a sandwich though often used more loosely for anything going with a cup of tea. See Char and Wad.

WAAF
Pronounced waff, a member of the Women's Auxiliary Air Force. Of enormous help in relieving men for service overseas and, very often, as attractive companions, there were some unfortunate (and untrue) things said about them, for instance this verse from an amateur concert party show at RAF Yatesbury in June 1942.

> The Waff, the Waff, the riff of the Raff,
> The flair force of the air force.'

Wallah

Person, another word from Hindustani. Those who served in India knew, amongst others, the char wallah who served tea from a charcoal heated urn, the pani wallah who carried the water containers, the dhobi wallah who did the laundry and the durzi wallah who was a tailor.

Weapon

Much hilarity was caused when, with the introduction of AI (Aerial interception or airborne radar used in night fighters to detect their quarry); there was a need to introduce new words into R/T code. Weapon, the euphemism for the male organ of gender (to quote the manual of RAF law), being used to describe the radar set. It was all the more humorous when used with the code words for serviceable and unserviceable, viz:

Control: *'Is your weapon flashing?'*
Pilot: *'No, my weapon is bent.'*

Clearly the senior officers who created these code words, intended to fox the enemy, must have had a wry smile on their faces when they devised these.

Weaving

What one had to get if hurry was required.
'Chiefy wants this job done yesterday, we'd better get weaving.'

Willco

A code word used in R/T communication following roger. *'Roger, willco'* indicating that not only had the message been received but that the recipient will comply with the instructions given.

Wingco

Sometime irreverently WC. Officer of Wing Commander rank. *See* Flush

Wizard Prang

Looking to the future, a well-contrived idea for a joke; looking back that the joke had come to a satisfactory conclusion. Also a term of congratulation for something successfully accomplished. A chap returns from leave and tells his mates that he got married: *'Wizard prang, old boy!'*

W/Op

Pronounced wop. A wireless operator, not to be mistaken for Italians, also called wops. Hence Wop/AG, wireless operator air gunner. All aircrew wireless operators were also trained as air gunners and initially wore the AG brevet. Later, warrant officer and commissioned Wop/AGs considered their extra training and skill was not adequately recognised since they did not wear the sparks badge; a new brevet S (for signaller) was introduced for all wop/AGs, only straight air gunners wearing the original AG brevet.

Works and Bricks

The Air Ministry Works Directorate. The department which handled the maintenance of buildings. In Britain they were the khaki clad airmen since their working 'uniform' was a two piece suit of denim overalls.

Jean Beadle, née Harris (1923–2000) was born and educated in Edinburgh. She volunteered for the WAAF in 1941 and was trained at Cranwell as a teleprinter operator.

Her first posting, to RAF Charterhall in Berwickshire, was fortuitous as it was there that she met her future husband. In 1943 she was posted to the Signals Centre at HQ 17 Group Coastal Command in Edinburgh where she remained until her demob in 1945. Returned to civilian life she worked as a clerk/typist in that city until the return home of her husband from Burma.

After having two children, when in 1963 her husband was appointed headmaster of a new school in Kenilworth, she became school secretary, a job from which she retired in 1984 after 21 years service. She died just a week into the millennium leaving two children Sandra and Ross and four grandchildren Tamsen, Adam, Eleanor and Joslyn.

Bernard Beadle was born in London in 1923. Wanting to fly, he joined the RAF in 1941 but was found to be colour blind so he trained at Blackpool and Yatesbury as a wireless operator.

His first posting was to RAF Charterhall, but in 1943 he joined one of the many mobile units in the 2nd Tactical Air Force being prepared for the impending 'Second Front'. Landing in Normandy on D+10 he followed in support of the advancing British and Canadian armies after the breakout through northern Europe. On VE Day he was posted back to Blighty, and had just enough time to marry Jean, before being shipped out to the Far East until March 1946.

After demob he trained as a teacher and worked in schools in Kent and Bedfordshire before being appointed to the first of his two deputy headships in Warwickshire. In 1963 he opened, as head, a new school in Kenilworth from which he retired in 1984. Since retirement he has continued his active membership of Rotary and of several ex-service organisations. His retirement hobbies are writing his memoirs when not building and operating his model railway.

Helping the Royal Air Force Benevolent Fund

By buying this book you are also contributing to the Royal Air Force Benevolent Fund.

The Royal Air Force Benevolent Fund was founded in 1919 by Lord Trenchard, just a year after he founded the Royal Air Force. He recognised a need to provide help and support to the veterans of the Great War, as well as to the families of those who would not return, and so he established what would become the RAFBF.

In that first year, the RAFBF gave £919 to relieve distress amongst members of the RAF Family and, more than 85 years on, its underlying mission remains to help people in the RAF Community who are in need.

Last year the Fund spent over £24 million to improve the lives of more than 30,000 members of the RAF Family who were facing difficulties. Such help is tailored to individual needs and is available to everyone who has entered into productive service in the RAF or any of its associated forces – regardless of age, rank or background – and their immediate dependants.

The RAFBF assists in many ways and can offer a broad range of help, including housing maintenance, provision of wheelchairs, specialist equipment and mobility aids. In some cases education costs and housing can also be provided.

The RAFBF also runs Princess Marina House in Sussex – offering respite breaks – and other establishments in partnership with the Royal Air Forces Association as well as having special arrangements with many more homes.

The Fund also supports other charities and groups that help our extended family, from hospices to playgroups for children with developmental difficulties. Those from other nations who served with or alongside the RAF are not forgotten either – the Fund's reach is truly international with awards reaching as far away as the Caribbean and Eastern Europe.

The RAFBF wants to reach out to members of the RAF Family who are in need and spread the message that the Fund is there to help them. A freephone number, 0800 169 2942, is available to make it easier for people to contact the Fund.